Thoughts Of Creativity King
114 Realities

By

Dorian Scott Withrow Jr.

To request permissions, contact the publisher at 114realities@gmail.com

ISBN

Paperback: 979-8-9865238-0-4

Hardcover: 979-8-9865238-1-1

Publisher: Dorian S. Withrow Jr./ Withrow LLC

"Learn all you can and apply your thoughts in any way.
Make gold from the dirt.
Make unclear springs transparent.
Enhance anyone in your path."

Dorian Scott Withrow Jr.

Acknowledgments:

Jessica Miller did fantastic work drawing images she conceived of through the poems she read. I want to thank everyone for the ideas, advice, and tips to enhance the book.

Follow
Instagram, Tik Tok, Snapchat: dswjr.18

Website
www.dswjr.com

Contact
Email: 114realities@gmail.com

Content

Why create this book?

I hope to inspire people and change their minds as they read. This is a creative self help book. A book which provides tools for mental fortitude, resilience, and a new outlook on life. There are life lessons and philosophies that can transform your lenses. A sad circumstance can be looked at differently to reach comfort. The poems provided can turn an angry emotion into a calm state. Whether for enjoyment, self-fulfillment, or life navigation, I want anyone reading this to get something out of it.

Free Verse

This book is a compilation of free verse that consist of life lessons and philosophy. Poetry is one of my passions and thought releases. It is an open form of poetry without a pattern. Literary devices are relevant to poetry because it is like adding seasoning to food. Literary devices can make poems tasteful, enjoyable, and complete.

Inspiration

The inspiration I gain comes from individual stories or conversations. In addition, lessons I come across in schooling, experiences, world events, and daily conversations. I encourage you to add notes to the pages to comment on the poetry. To bring forth new ideas, I want you to address your likes and dislikes. Get a separate sheet of paper to write your own poetry. Think about how you may be able to apply this to your life or poetic work.

Literary devices

Allusion- Expression of something to mind without saying it.
Diction- Word Choices or use of words or phrases in speech.
Euphemism is a word or expression used to substitute for one considered harsh, embarrassing, or unpleasant.
Foreshadow-warning or indication.
Imagery- Visual description.
Rhyme- Sounds between or at the end of words.
Metaphor- Comparing something without using like or as.
Simile- Comparing something using "like" or "as."
Personification- Attribute or characteristic to something non-living.
Allegory- Story used to represent real-life experience.
Alliteration- Series of words or phrases that start with the same sound, usually consonants.
Colloquialism- Informal language or slang.
Hyperbole- exaggeration.
Irony- Statement used to express the opposite meaning.
Juxtaposition- Comparing and contrasting two or more different things.
Onomatopoeia- Use words that represent a sound.
Repetition- Repeating a word or phrase.
Synecdoche- Something used to represent a whole.

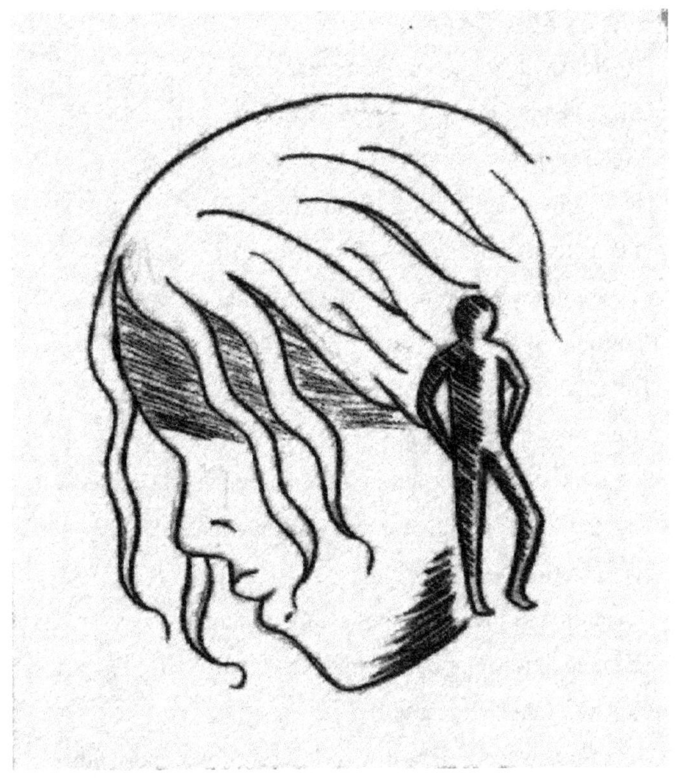

Illustration by Jessica Sade Miller

Another Love Poem

Unwieldy, slow, heavy, and pale as lead.
Unwieldy, the mass of her beauty.
Slow was her every step,
Heavy, the weight of her kindness.
Pale as lead, the way I feel when she is not around.
The sound of her voice was the best tune
The sight of her was beyond any feeling.
Time spent causes me to peel my shell away.
I loved her hair, sleek & so fine.
She looked so good; putting on makeup was a sacrilege.
Together as a collective, there was happiness in every conversation.
Priceless was the smile she would give me.
She made me smile back, almost as if she controlled me.
I loved it when she teased me.
Her music was foreign; it was different from many others
Not a day went by when being together was boring.
The worst times together were when the times were brief
Those times were like being between a rock and a hard place.
Her weirdness & questions brought my great wall down
She led me to open up a little.
I opened the cover so she could read my interests, likes & dislikes.
In return, I questioned her to do the same
Got her likes & dislikes, her amazing interests.
I like being near her.

I dislike being away from her.
It was like my greatest dislikes were the days when she wasn't around.
I wanted her, a connection like fingers & folding,
Babies & holding, bees' & honey, thieves & money.
Being together would've been cool.
But to get her was another story.

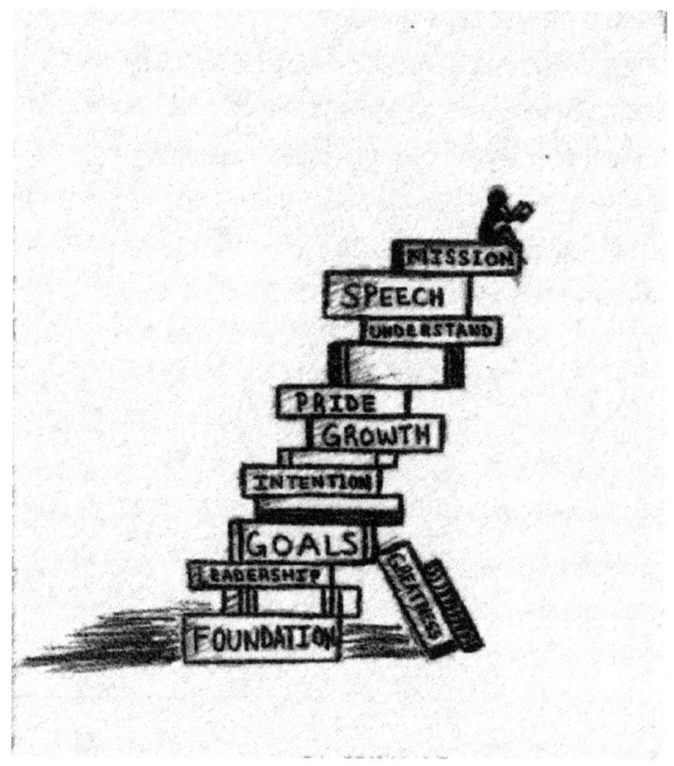

Illustration by Jessica Sade Miller

A Goal of Mine

Part of my mission is to become the greatest role model.
Someone your children would follow.
An example any adult can admire.
People deep in the holes will see greater height.
People deep in the holes will find footing to climb out.
People will gain the vision to handle grooves to reach their way out.
Everyone has their hole.
Everyone has their climb.
I want to become a positive influence.
I'm someone you will read in the books.
Someone you'll look at and go blind by my shine.
I feel that my purpose is to create a moral society.
Do great things for my family and the people surrounding me.
To have other people follow in similar footsteps.
Pave the way for future generations.
Hope that a cycle of great legacy continues.
I want to be remembered for positive change itself.
I want to be remembered for success.
I want to be remembered for self productivity.
I want to be remembered for progress.
A goal of mine.

Illustration by Jessica Sade Miller

Apocalypse

The end of the world will not be zombies.

It will be fear, death of careers, and unmoving gears.

Giant loss of labor.

Lost lives are not just bullets.

Loss of meaning is a loss of life.

War is not only battling another country.

War is also citizens battling each other.

Food shortage is far.

Most of the country's bodies are abundant.

Picky and greed combined; make an atomic bomb.

Picky about people, greedy about green-faced and coded paper.

Some people get off pretending to be a klutz.

This led to some cuts in the gut for not keeping a mouth shut.

But with luck, you won't have to keep your chin tucked.

Distrust might take out more segregation than anything else.

It'll be hard to keep your head up; it's better than a head down.

Bow when you meet respect, but wave when you regret.

Out LOUD!

Fear is a powerful breaking tool.
Afraid of speaking,
I can be pretty loud,
Although some things can lead me to be silent.
Anything hard to say is not said but written.
For me, a speech may be a breeze.
Spoken words on stage will make me appear like a kitten.
Speaking up was a challenge...scratch that still.
But my best true excuse is that I'm soft-spoken.
Confidence was not in question for speaking.
Nay, It is a question for speaking out about this or that.

Illustration by Jessica Sade Miller

Unrealistic Relaxation

Something I always wanted was a state of continuous peace & prosperity.

A place where relaxation & kindness become addictions.

When my mind is led to what troubles me,

I hit a relapse that comes with bags all under my eyes.

While sleep is difficult, imagination is strong.

I sit with my legs crossed, my head sinks deeply.

Eyelids that feel as if they weigh a thousand pounds,

When I rest, I hope to keep them closed for a long time.

Through this state, I control a different reality.

I enter a dream-like utopia.

A place where kindness prevails while cruelty vanishes.

I dream of an unrealistic hope, though.

What a pessimistic thought?

Maybe I can gain the power to turn back time.

Move into the past, and change it for the better.

Maybe this can be my present.

I'd be devoid of hearing about people's precious liquid increasing in absence.

In addition to a tax paid assassin, intentional food poisoning, deadly medication,.

In this space, I make terrors that haunt everyone speechless.

This place holds great people's paradise.

Having fun rolling a par-a-dice.

Money isn't my measure of wealth but my internal richness.

Maybe I can blow the imaginary numbers into the air to better enrich others.
Rejection of material things to gain richness.
Put this heavy, dirty yellow, shiny rock back into the earth.
This reality, a hope for a formula.
This place multiplies happiness, adds unity, avoids division, and stops subtracting the family.
This place maintains positive signs without tangents and is devoid of quintessential paradigms.
Grouping up and eliminating risk factors that increase negative probability.
This calculation is hope; it provides an answer to peace.

Insecurities

Poor thoughts follow me like a stray.

It sits on either shoulder like good and evil.

It's like carrying heavy iron buckets of water while walking a tightrope.

Two magnetic walls on either side.

I am not allowed to let a drop fall.

Far, far below, there is a pool of sadness and anger.

Positive reminders are like a drain.

A good ear can take the walls away,

Take some advice, never pick up the buckets.

Avoid the cause of it; you may never walk the rope.

Illustration by Jessica Sade Miller

The Peacock

He heavily loathes blindness but adores being seen by all.
Desire for attention is the mass of the sun, moon, and everything else in the dark void.
Wrist that flashes so bright it may blind retinas.
His neck is as thick as the hulks from the gold ring and diamonds.
People are in awe, attention to a crisp, unwrinkled, stainless buttoned shirt.
Socks, tall, white with polka dots, shiny black shoes, and black slacks so slick it will make dust resist.
All these externals to get heads turning.
This may be okay, although there is a negative to a positive.
To put others down by bragging about it is not humble.
All those material things just to show people mental limitations.
His eyes developed a sight of arrogance hierarchy.
How could he let the money do this?
In the end,
You are not your money,
Your clothes,
Your jewelry.
You are not what people say about you.
You are who you think you are.

Illustration by Jessica Sade Miller

Fear

I'm taking a trip down memory lane.

Looking back, I feel proud of my past.

In the lane I walked; I feared the cement would not like every inch of my foot.

I feared people passing by would insult me behind my back.

What low self-esteem?

I felt people did not like the smile on my face when they looked at it.

Eye contact made me queasy, and contact with people was not easy.

My legs are weakening from insecurities.

I don't know if I can finish this trip.

I don't know if this poem would give me a definition.

Another fear is not finishing the trip.

At the pinnacle of my embarrassments, I would turn into euphoria.

If I feared people in general, who would not be threatening to me?

How vulnerable.

If I could not finish my thought,

If I could not complete eye contact,

If I could finish being so low and talk louder,

If I could only stop stuttering and finish my sentences,

If I could not finish the day walking upright and confidently,

Then I've become prey.

I’ve opened the door to be walked on and treated terribly like some doormat.
Looking back, I wish I’d gone blind, but this trip influenced security.
Now I laugh at it; that walk made me the strong individual I am today.
The best joke ever created.

The Playboy

You do it all blatant.

If only you could hear the names, people called you,

Maybe they're just names you have created yourself.

No matter how silly, opinions do not make you.

No matter what I say, I see you are careless.

These women use your words to mock you like a parrot.

These beautiful birds take your words to make a song out of them.

You are mad at them for giving you proper defamation.

Look at them, Einstein; you do not have to be smart to figure it out.

The people that do not think always get caught up.

You admire them from a distance, close the gap.

You toss a bunch of slick myths in their face.

You keep it short; lies fall in order.

You put on a rich front with little funds.

Say whatever to get some, leave them after like a medical glove.

A bunch of lies may get you stuck in a hole.

You have burrowed your way down; I know you probably noticed that.

Now you are stuck with a babe.

What use is a crib when the child is at a distance?

Become custom with arguments about custody.

Money is the grandmaster of motivation.

Child support is the kicker.

The child may get punches from both sides.

That human being was knocked out by two fighters only using words.

Playboy, you have to live with that.

Know how to be calm and patient.

Illustration by Jessica Sade Miller

Daily Costume

What is beauty to me?

You are crazy gorgeous.

Is there better hair than your own?

I accept any texture you offer.

The fans you call lashes could not cool you off.

You've devalued your face with the unnatural.

When it is off, do you feel worthless?

You may have found it all worthless.

By using those substances, you cover flawless creation.

What is pretty, attractive, and beautiful?

You communicate a lot of fear through contacts.

The view of beauty can break by external means.

Going broke in self-esteem dollars leads to corruption in identity.

What makes you-you?

Do not use things to make what is already magnificent worse.

Makeup is applied, and treatment is to fix the damage makeup causes.

Then we have more makeup to cover that up.

There is a constant cycle of unnecessary money loss.

Aging is hidden, only to look worse than the past.

In the end, you look for pleasure in the mirror.

How do you feel when you take the costume off?

A little Ego

I believe in providing myself with inward delight.
It will be hard for people to take it from you.
The longest-standing finger could not rob you.
I have a scotoma in that type of sign language.
I don't consider it ignorance or any offense.
I refuse to be controlled by others.
I avoid many people because I detect disgrace.
Some believe that's not the way to think about
I think I'm above that standard.
I just thought that some are still.
The still is without change.
I avoid this stillness.
My mental ego runs, sometimes tripping because it did not crawl.
Maybe running caused me to be dismissive.
I think that caused me to murder possible relationships.
I'm searching for a phoenix.

Illustration by Jessica Sade Miller

Self Love

I love myself.
Sometimes it hurts when reaching for it.
That in itself is salt on a wound.
I expect the most out of myself; I try to treat myself the best.
There is a difference between I try and will.
Sometimes I fail at the I will; therefore, I will try.
If I keep trying, I will not reach it.
I unintentionally hurt myself.
I teach myself right, and I think of myself to be like a flashlight.
With that in mind, I should have an internal fight.
Self-esteem built on externals is slight to yourself; keep satisfaction inward.
Construct positive pillars on aspects of yourself; confidence follows.
You'll lose the need for outside desire validation.
This validation leads to a trivial clout chase.
It's all in your head; this abstraction that should've been abandoned.
Develop a fine peace of mind and avoid vice.
Don't be consumed by compliments.
If you do, then all they say is what you think instead of what you think.
A reflection of what makes you great should not be interpreted by other people.
Now I contemplate what my reflection is.

I have to develop the best pictures of myself in my mind.

Naturally selected, I realized I couldn't be replicated.

Illustration by Jessica Sade Miller

Wolf and Sheep

Wolves cannot fake smart sheep.

Dumb sheep are caught through deception.

If sheep know sheep, then they are less likely to get caught.

If sheep understood wolves, they would not be prey.

If wolves know sheep, the wolves will not go hungry.

Existence

Potential is one of the greatest possibilities.

The future is nebulous, and so is its potential.

My existence was rejected before I could have a breath to defend my place here.

What I have placed here has led rejection to appreciation.

Doors continuously open, so I gladly walk through each.

Each time, I come out with a different human being.

Those same people will claim some part of my breath.

Smile when my…

Hug when my…

Laugh when my…

Eyes shine; you can see the sun on their face when my breath comes.

They acknowledge my accomplishment.

Their hearing reaches the level of a bat when I give council.

Annihilation before my breath would have been insane.

Do not be crazy enough to consider under pressure.

Premonition

I came to the house unannounced while I made some rounds.
I was greeted with pleasant kindness.
Whenever I see her in this state, my thoughts aren't the best.
We were talking about experiences throughout the summer so far.
I was cut short in my explanation.
I was told I have some paperwork for you.
So confused; I did not have a clue.
Life insurance involves me; I'm a beneficiary.
I kind of froze,
I wasn't expecting it.
I just said okay, but I was in dismay.
I was upset because I did not want money.
I want a longer life for you.
Sooner or later, these thoughts always crept.
Most of the time, I don't want to believe it.

Rock

Bind to my emotionless appearance.

On the outside, it is easy to fake a smile.

I keep it all in my head.

People might call me a robot.

I'm not the type to be put in a pot; I hate being mixed with others.

Worry solves nothing; no need to panic.

Be phlegmatic to avoid any disturbance.

I'm not empty, but

I have an abundance to solve.

My list of problems is long; I'm not taught how to manage them.

I think I'm hurting.

I think I'd just keep a scotoma to the issues.

I have involuntarily raised the issues on the list.

I wish I could abort negative emotions.

These past feelings made me who I am today, so I embrace them.

I try not to overthink.

When I tell others, will they listen?

I wondered If the concern was even serious.

I'll continue my memory loss until reminders come back.

I'll just write it down.

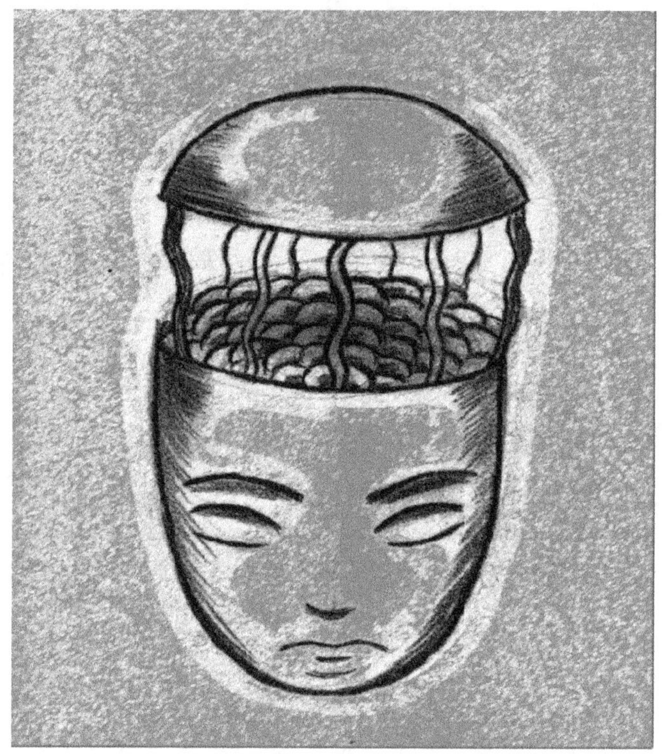

Illustrated by Jessica Sade Miller

Conflicting decisions

Should I stay, or should I go?

This choice might end in sorrow.

My thoughts are static, and questioning seems silly.

People lash out then; morals aren't backed now.

Sometimes it is hard to know right or left.

I did not mean right or wrong.

Decisions in a pinch make the skin peel.

Wrong actions can be the best option for a good outcome.

The opposite of right is even better.

From what I know, there is always a choice.

The appropriate action tends to be the hardest.

Maybe the longest, but the safest.

A decision can pull a cover off a blank canvas.

Action makes the painting.

Masterminds

Sensical words to a nonsensical mind don't make sense.

This nonsense they call “nuts,”

A teacher tries to bury it for a perspective to be dug up later.

Unfortunately, I do not know why some people do not find what is buried.

They are not dumb or crazy; rather see them as lazy.

People refuse to dig.

To this day, they amaze me, yet, I’m numb to their sight.

When eyes are glazy, one is blind to exposed light in dark areas.

Some mentality blocks light to stay in a dark area they trip in.

People come out of a blind hole with a shovel when the sense is sought.

When sense is reached, desires move towards a world of cultivation.

When cultivation is reached one resides in a space of separation.

Trust

Ignorance is deception's closest relative.

A kind heart can be a thief's greatest jewel.

If the little things have to be camouflaged, I'm scared of what is invisible.

Enough encounters with a cheat will lead you to reconsider honesty.

Our societal conditions will make it so.

Miscommunication will lead to a bad interaction.

Miscommunication will lead to mistrust between the trustworthy.

Foresight can help produce more trust and put skepticism on a decline.

Trust is having a win for people on both sides.

Forgiveness for dishonesty is good.

But…

It is better not to be cut at all than place a bandage over a wound.

Some Of Our Relationships

In a lot of lives, connections are not existent.

Everyone is in a situation they control.

Puppet to a past mentality.

There is a cycle-

The next grew resentment towards the past and passed it on.

Conflicted with how to treat a spouse or a pleasure piece.

Both could be broken; both feel fixed when they have each other.

Someone to someone else lost value.

Truth is the most craved unwanted idea.

Arguments build a fence.

Sometimes they hop the fence to fix a vase they dropped together.

On either side of the fence, both should have made the grass greener.

Desired behavior

It is both natural and learned.

Positive behavior needs positive praise.

Give rose up front, not in secret.

Sometimes you will have to take away to reach the goal.

Repetition is key.

Association unlocks a powerful mentality.

It sets a correlation between good action and wanted consequence.

Fighting Song

Music can consist of vocals.

Songs have notes.

There are genres with differences within them.

Everyone makes a different song.

Martial arts has its own song.

Martial arts have different styles, different genres.

Each style has different techniques, different notes.

Everyone has a different style.

Listen to the song, the music will flow through your body.

A sing-along.

Must have both

Causality rules.

There cannot be a good without bad.

For there to be disrespect, there must be respect.

There is something not so funny in laughter.

Honor and disgrace have a connection.

To have compassion, there must be heartlessness.

For happiness to exist, there must be sadness.

Fortune and misfortune are in bondage.

When there is a win, there is a loss.

Leaders always have followers.

Strength and weakness exist in the same place.

Alliances form to combat enemies.

Where there are locks, there are thieves.

When abundance is present, sharing holds a greater presence.

Love and hate coexist all interchangeably.

Nothing is certain when we live in constant flux.

Simple

Simple things go a long way.

You taught me patience,

You taught me perseverance,

You taught me to work smarter.

You taught me to work hard at being smarter.

You taught me you do not have to be the smartest.

You taught me to be the wisest.

You taught me not every lesson has to be hard.

You taught me to learn the easy way.

You taught me to learn the ways of the hard way, but follow the easy way.

You taught me not to follow in their footsteps.

You taught me to learn from the older ones.

You told me to follow my gut or whatever is speaking to me.

Sleep

Luxury mattress,
It can be compared to a baby in a loving mother's arms.
The most expensive bed sheets and blanketed with the best material.
Alright, now I've gotta have the best sleep.
The room is dark and without a whisper.
Keep the anger high and let demons creep in.
A happy homeless man will have a happier life than you.
Sorrow is another self-propagating product perpetually produced in the worry factory.
Check the emotions because they can make sleep harder.
Not much can beat a good night's sleep.
I say this candidly: you can't buy sanity.
Misery loves company.
Money might be your best guess.
You don't trust a soul is my best guess.

Little

When less is seen,

Open your eyes to how little you need.

Not need but want.

Fault arrives when wants become needs.

Excuses can construct a road to disaster.

If you have everything you need, you'll have more than most.

Take a trip to triple what you know.

Come back, you will see how much you grow.

I Like You

I don't like you,

I don't like your breath.

It smells fresh...

I don't like your clothing,

It matches and without wrinkles,

The insult burns; I ironed out words.

I don't like your jewelry,

It has a pretty cool shine.

It's not just gonna shine, it'll blind you too.

You're ugly.

I'm my top model.

The difference between your insult and compliment is a fine line.

I chose what I wanted to hear.

Barely Learned To Cope

No one is perfect?

I do not believe anyone has seen perfect.

Maybe it is in our face and all around us, we just don't know it.

We were made in the image of the inconceivable.

Some prefer the image of something else.

The big concern is self and some loathe it.

Lung chokers and lethal liver liquids.

These leave your brain's litmus test very blue.

Life in the blues is not a pleasant one.

Health detrimental comforters are the worst cushion.

Take care of your health and you may reach a new mood.

Meditation, guidance, exercise, and reading inspiration.

Embrace it and take away the basic blues.

Self-help, don't go crazy on dope.

Please learn to cope.

Those From Stars

We come from the sun and nature,
The first and most advanced standard of mankind.
The sun rays and skin,
Like water and sponge.
Eyes plunged in gold, they had rich sight.
Some lived their lives lavishly.
Some had battles, weapons and martial arts.
They ate from plates,
They had the mental strength of a diamond.
They were ballers, globe trotted around the world.
Some scored and shared the wealth,
They worked together as a team
And opposed each other as family would.
The only opposition were themselves,
Through differences, they worked together.
In division, their chemistry declined,
The team fell apart.

Story Toppers

The greatest human asset is fallibility.

We all like to tell stories for willing ears.

Stories of adversity, advancement or adjustment are adequate.

One oughta quit the negative stores.

Negative stories bring back lost indignation.

Listening ear will add in, one anger turns to two.

A bunch of complaints and a turbulent atmosphere.

It can even become a competition.

Who had it worse, who was more infuriating, what measure of sadness?

Beating a dead horse will not bring it back to life.

It will continue rotting.

I Learned

We rushed, feelings were powerful.

Red flags were waving, but I couldn't see their color.

I rushed out of the gate mindlessly with direction.

I wanted to learn, I just wanted to see what it would be like.

I did not know what I wanted from it.

While in it, I realized it's not desirable.

Emotions and attraction kept me there.

Kept me in this thing I thought was love.

I was not content and I put myself into a prison.

I didn't want you, but wanted what we had.

I still feel bad.

So I left you while you were still with me.

I ended up going back and forth between staying and leaving.

We both became bitter.

It's hard to converse now.

The truth came out in the end.

Her

My lady, my muffin, and too many names to mention.
My Smiles are harder to hide in your presence.
The time we spend is unbelievable but believe this.
These words are hard to form, so I write.
Even when silent, you read me like a psychic.
As each other sidekicks, we defeat our internal villains,
Whether caged up to be released later or exterminated.
Anyway, your smile relieves the pain,
Insecurity subsides when I hold you in my arms.
Your affection blinds me to the world like a bear mace.
That may not be the best analogy but analyze this.
Love is abstract and it can be defined a billion different times.
To each its own, I think when you know, you know.
We aren't in anyone's head, so who's to say.
Know my feelings are true.
I love you.

Ks

I don't understand you.
Judging by what you stand for, I suppose you don't understand me either.
I sit here to make these words stand out.
You persist in planting evil seeds.
You reap what you sow.
Dark acts light up your points.
I would like to point out that we are not threatening.
Too brainwashed for that.
We want to live.
You follow God's word and praise demonic acts
Convinced that those demons are angels.
I call these your young recruits.
On top of that, there are lies and manipulation.
Like a big puppet show.
Pulling strings to make life harder for the imaginary opposition.
We aren't enemies.
Some of us see illusions shown.
To some, they don't appear at all.
Even if it's faint, you'll see the light from the dark
Your sow is close.

Visionaries

The thought of the end goal is great.
Where is the start?
Where is the plan?
The work usually seems to be subtracted,
All bark, but no bite.
Speeches and preaching are like a seed.
Where is the water, proper temperature and sunlight?
There must be the right soil combined with the best PH.
This is a big problem in the development of the plant.
We have control over conditions to make goals possible.
Organization and cooperation are a big problem.
The useless efforts and methods are always put in.
The strong methods are overlooked.
Effort that takes a lot of time is terrifying.
Money is a fast solution as well as a great fix illusion.
A lot of factors will harm the plant's development.
The plant is not there yet
Let the final product reveal itself.

Your Thoughts

A man I've met only a few, barely knew.
As I think back to when I was about the height of a yard stick,
Your presence is blurry.
Not until recently, thoughts came like a flurry.
I've heard of him as time passed.
Searching through the blizzard, my eyes became clearer.
A man that battled in a jungle during a Vietnam war.
A blood I never knew, only through oral stories.
The last time we met, communication was only visual.
I wondered what you thought.
What do you make of this almost unrecognizable teen?
I did not know what to say or how to feel.
I could not produce anything for someone I did not know.

Parochialism

No idea is better than your own.
Everyone else's ideas aren't ideal.
It is not worth understanding.
What is in your mind is absolute.
Why listen to anyone else-
They are all wrong, you are always right.
Only words of significance are mine alone.
I don't walk alone.
Shoot their perspective full of holes.
Disagree and yell till they see my side.
Why see varying views? It does not agree with me.
No idea is better than my own.

Unlocked

Where there are locks, there are thieves.

We share when there is abundance.

We withhold when there is absence.

If value places on material things and economic gain, bad things come.

Scarcity develops desperation and reduction delays gratification.

Tomorrow is a mystery and the poor's behavior makes rules.

If you control resources, then you control behavior.

You can push any ideas you want and advocate any laws you desire.

Those ideas and laws are beautiful to the eyes that have seen ugly.

Images can speak in greater volumes than anything.

There is no issue if people see no issue.

There is freedom, even comfort when people do not know.

Asceticism is bound to nationalism.

They are the free people although they are just as cages as the zoos they visit.

To those who see the image of freedom, knowing an unlocked cage will change life dramatically.

We all do what is in our best interest.

Family

A song can run smoothly and when it does, no notes stand out.

Mistakes happen and when they do, good notes stand out.

We acknowledge the good notes and consider the rest rubbish.

We make an exception for them.

The notes even fall and sometimes are forgotten.

I believe in maintaining every note until there are no mistakes.

There will always be mistakes; that is why we practice to reduce them.

Our job is to enhance the notes when we interact with them.

Blood is said to be greater than water, but money can supersede both.

Education in ethics and morality can combat all.

Selfishness, greed and negative priorities can break the song.

Village

It takes a village to raise a child.
Mind your own business brought the business to you.
Generational ignorance is a thing-
Some parents never got that light bulb to "ding".
We are learning, but let's do it together.
The wrong ones got a hold of the young ones.
Those who know better do better.
Knowing better does not always mean getting involved.
The people who "know better" can be as bad as the ignorant.
The snow on their doorstep is not a problem until it comes to yours.
Smoke is not a problem until you get choked.
Now smoke has gotten your irritated attention like getting poked.
Maybe they need a word of advice.
Seeing is believing, so live it.
Make sure your own child is straight.
Parents need checking too.
their stories can be pretty blue.
Help them get a few clues.

Correction

They ruled unwisely.

Warlords fell to greed.

Business handled with the wrong people.

The land was rich and novel, so largely, theft was not code

Selfishness did not thrive.

Spiritual belief was not enough

Tradition of giving and acceptance.

Social codes only for peace.

Tyrants did not dictate.

Comparison

I have seen the affluence make fun of those with less.
Poke a joke at the ones that wear less.
Disgust at what they eat,
Confusion towards their creed and rituals.
Not everything is understood, but respect is needed.
To the affluent I have questions;
What if your electricity disappeared?
Clean water, gone?
What if grocery stores vanished?
Gasoline is no longer available.
Terrible transformation of law and order.
Communication and anger will set in.
You'll be like the scavenging rats you dislike so much.
Hunger so deep you might chew on bugs.
Cold nights and hot days you can't escape.
The stench of body order can match a skunk.
Conditions that'll make a saint a sinner.

The Sage

The sage is always teachable; ears are always open.
The sage is all accepting.
Every voice matters to this being.
The sage knows what is internal is what matters most.
Predatorial eyes can take away gifts instilled since birth.
Societal benefactors, the more pure demonstration of righteousness.
A sage does not fight for class or trample others.
Value on what is important can prevent robbery.
The sage lives in a way that magnetizes the good.
Good people, our earthly relatives, and fortune.
Fortune is not limited to material resources.
The sage rid itself of arrogance as time dwindles.
Sage's intense tolerance.
The sage will attempt to make a bond with the dog that bit him.
When practicing discipline, balance between extremes is best.
The sage knows what is weak.
The appearance of strength can be awfully fragile.
Pride from wins can bring losses.
Losses can help people gain pride to win.
Bad, unfair competition.
All trust begins with trusting yourself,
Follow through with your word.
Speak so all words are valuable.

Live virtuously.

World of pleasures

What is a world of pleasures?

Internally or externally?

Can a child living a life of hell know anything else?

Can a child that lives a life of heaven know worse?

Too much pleasure and enjoyment become dull.

A life in tragedy has to experience pleasure internally.

But for how long?

When living in luxury, pleasure is external.

When luxury is lost, so is pleasure.

The child living in heaven may be forced to seek happiness internally.

The child living in hell may be forced to seek happiness externally.

Bridges

You never know which bridge you'll have to cross.

Life is like a fighting match; each attack thrown is a problem you'll defend.

Not everything can be blocked or evaded.

Some things are unexpected.

A good support system can combat this.

Sometimes we are not ready no matter how much anyone prepares.

Bridges are those support systems for attacks.

Without bridges, anyone is likely to lose the match.

Attacks are unpredictable and so is fire.

We wish the fire never started.

Force

Force is a false sense of power.

Force is morally corrupt and corrosive.

Force can lead to irritation, indignation, and exasperation.

Force leads to invoking anger.

The consequence of force is a lack of courtesy.

Force is murder.

Force is squeezing resources.

Force is laws and policies to put people under.

Force is putting people against each other.

Force is manipulation.

The Race Fallacy

Genetics, history, anthropology and more should have made it clear.

Human existence should have made it obvious.

Ignorable creates a nebulous sight.

Ignorance creates silly fights.

This ignorance created pain.

The stubborn refuse truth and evidence when information is given.

Books are somehow obsolete when people are strong in their options.

Certain knowledge creates an antithesis among people.

This is not a rejection of color.

I accept all differences, but we come first.

It is these physical differences that make us even more similar.

Prayers

Prayers are always answered.

It may not be what we think.

Prayers are not always answered in the way we would like.

Prayer could have been answered this whole time.

Change perspective!

You will see that your prayers have come to fruition.

Irrelevant Importance

Those who got struck by lightning received great rewards.

Those same people will tell you passion and hard work can get you struck too.

Most want to get struck, but advice like that can leave them stuck.

This false sense of hope is a generational curse.

The more they idolize the people who were struck, the worse it gets.

The idolized are an awfully good distraction for bad issues.

We are often better at finding a solution to reach a championship than real problems.

More concerned with a draft pick than eliminating the cause for people to hit licks.

Concern for shooting a basketball is more relevant than gun violence.

The new album holds more weight than verbal abuse.

The best fight takes away focus from domestic violence.

We might go to the hall of fame for being literally priceless.

Knowledge is suffering

A person is conscious of ills.

A person aware of horrific conditions.

The experience of problems in reality.

When a person knows things can be better, it hurts inside.

One of the biggest steps to solving a problem comes through awareness.

When you solve it for yourself, you are better able to help someone else.

Someone who knows the subject best is able to teach it.

Words are not enough, action needs its place.

Be that moral exemplar.

Vulnerability

There is a certain power to opening up.

Metaphorically open up your chest.

Do this and you'll experience a type of freedom.

A freedom many do not and will not have.

Open up and so will they.

Give an honest cry; they will let down waterfalls.

Express your world; wait to receive theirs.

Using vulnerability for evil is inconceivable.

A good heart is feasible.

Keep in line and anyone is keepable.

Argue

If they are not reasonable,
They will get loud, they will insult.
If they feel slighted, then get ready!
They will be your worst artist.
Your words will be manipulated to suits their unjustifiable incompetence.
Rejection of honesty is repeated and refused.
You have burned their side to ashes.
They will resent, sometimes without repent.
Some would rather know less than more.
In the end, there are terrible feelings.
Neither side sees the other better from the start.
Do not argue, instead teach.

Immortality

You will live on because we will remember you.

I share your blood, so you live with me.

I took on your wisdom, so your thoughts live through me.

One last conversation is what I hoped for.

I poured my heart out in hopes that you understood me.

A release of air may have been my acknowledgement.

Many tears have come till this point and more after this.

A long cry after every talk.

My eyelids held tears back like a powerful damn.

My pain is not selfish.

My pain is the loss of someone.

A loss I cannot control.
Unrecognizable before transition.
Unrecognizable in the permanent white bed.
A bed topped with red and white roses.
A bed that lay in the creator's brown earth.
Your words will live on and so will I.
You will never die.

Forgiveness

I read a quote by Gandhi, it addressed forgiveness.

I still do not know where I live on this spectrum.

It is hard thinking about the past and how much it affects the present.

Who knows I probably would be writing about this in the present.

According to Gandhi, the strong forgive.

Here after all the muscle gain, I am still as weak as I was at the start.

In spite of you, I look for the answers to my questions.

Maybe self-perfection,

Maybe a public benefactor,

Maybe I can crank all morality into my cranium.

I am getting closer to forgiveness when I realize the conditions around me.

I become more grateful when I listen to stories.

Love you but I hate your actions.

But…

You taught me what taking care of your family looks like.

You taught me to go the extra mile.

You taught me that sacrifices need to be made.

You taught me to take care of my business.

You taught me to take care of my wife.

We all have problems.

Reaching for forgiveness eats me alive.

H.M.D

Looks aren't everything.

How empty would I be if looks were my focus?

I just have something to be proud of when I look in the mirror.

Whenever I am complimented, I take some of it on behalf of her.

I put in the work, but it could not have been without her.

I would not be the man I am today without her.

I have a lot to be grateful for and that is an understatement.

Love is always present like the sun and the moon.

Without her, life would have been a great mess.

Every decision has led up to this point.

I do not regret a single choice.

Bystander

So many faces, I become invisible.

Too many eyes,

What If I mess up?

Someone else might jump in.

I won’t have a responsibility then.

If I make a mistake, I will be responsible then.

If so many people weren’t around, I'd be more likely to put a hand in.

Categories

Some are prone to violence.
Some are known for peace.
Some are known to be thieves.
It might be their nature, it may be their place.
Generalizations make many, the few.
Most are prone to violence.
Most are known for peace.
Most are known to be thieves.
Most are faceless with little distinction.

Tests

Tests are not suited for everyone.

Everyone has a different design.

Everyone needs a different design.

For the people who have the knowledge to pass down.

The people in the affluent first world country.

The people who speak the language.

Those who have it the best are them.

There are exceptions to barriers.

Vocabulary, reading, arithmetic,

Not all have learned or learned well enough.

The barriers are seemingly endless.

But familiarity can change the game.

Enough time practicing will place progress in prominence.

Different methodologies in classrooms can make a way.

B.M.I.P.S

I have to be stern for you.
I have to smile for you.
I have to laugh for you.
I am a little nervous around you.
I have to cross the street for you.
I have a nod when passing you.
Then I would be less threatening to you.
I need standard English to be accepted by you.
I need ebonics so you're a little more comfortable.
Hands out of pocket for you.
No hoody on for you.
I have to be loud for you.
Don't be too loud for you.
I am clean, you know.
Apparently, I have drugs, to you.
You know I worked to wear this.
You said I had to sling to wear this.
You're proud of me.
The even more shocking part is that I can spell it.

Grateful

We don’t bless the food when it's easy to come by.
Diet restrictions go out the window when hunger comes.
You don’t pray so much when things go right.
When the world falls apart, your knees bleed.
When you can do no wrong, why ask for forgiveness?
From taboo to a barrage of begging.
When things go bad, you put everything out like a show and tell.

Wasted Time

Using my time to pass time.
Closed mouths don’t get fed.
Closed mouths don't feed either.
I asked questions like I expected the truth.
We could wash our hands of this mess,
But I would rather let this sink in.

Play

We play less as we age.
The variability is status or circumstances.
When there is more free time,
We can increase our youth on our decline.
A life more relaxing with more time to play.
More play can take away from old age.
There may be less enjoyment and more stiffness.
Can you imagine a mobile human forming into a gargoyle?
A sweet, colorful fruit gone bitter and gray.
We may lose a little color, but let's keep it sweet.

Revenge

The greatest human asset is fallibility.
The key is a comeback.
Unlocking success, it is the greatest revenge.
Listen to what you can be proud of.
Leave revenge in divine hands.
I was made in its image.
Gaze upon meeting your goal maker.
A bar that couldn't be reached.
A student that can teach.
Let me preach;
If I duplicated you in me, then I'd reduce myself.
I did not elevate to fall down.

Age

What did not make sense at a young age does now.

At ten, I realized I didn't need a lot of friends.

At twelve, I realized my temporary experience is shared by many.

At fourteen, I noticed the importance of a functional two-parent home.

At fifteen, education became much more important.

At sixteen, the ball started rolling down the lane of achievements.

At seventeen, I noticed life is not so pretty.

At eighteen, it became harder to deal with congratulations.

At nineteen, more effort meant alienation from life.

At twenty, questions were greater than before.

At twenty one, there is a lot of introspective work.

At twenty two, I have a head start and a good start.

Anger is a nuisance by twenty three. I want it to be prevented.

By twenty five, jealousy won't be a bump in the road.

By thirty, I should be living well off my gifts.

By forty, I hope to have everything I wanted.

By fifty, maybe my name is on track for legacy.

By Sixty, my desires might fade.

By seventy, I hope the youth learn from me.

By eighty, I hope I reach my heaven here first.

By ninety, I want to reach my century.

Teachable

This person asked me about a subject.

The person wants to know what I know.

There might be something I missed in my learning.

Listen attentively; fill any gaps in my knowledge.

Learning is everything to me.

My pleasure is getting to know all I can know.

Painter

I can create what I want.

Whatever size I can conceive in mind.

Whatever length can be measured.

You see any color I choose.

The object I draw can twist, curve, and loop.

It can play tricks and treat onlookers through optical illusion.

Art can be the greatest deception and present a great depiction.

Art may expose the flaws of our mind.

Art influences emotion, widens eyes, and makes speedy hearts.

It is almost like a dream come true.

I can make any appearance into existence.

I create all and anything that can be thought of.

The Poet

My honor sits in the reality of my words.
My desire is work edged in stone.
The memory of words sticks like my own name.
Even if I do not make a penny, the wealth of change is worth it.
Reverence is not my success.
Success is when others succeed too.
If the masses are down, then my success is none.
There is no "I" in team neither in "we" nor in "me".
The purpose of this is to run evils out.
As time passes, this flower grows with a bright bloom.
Everything outside of the message is spices in this recipe.
Flavor to my food and a taste which has never been acknowledged.
Sometimes I wonder if I should write some of these.
A vast sum of these is a recollection of the past.
Some of this remembrance brought tears, fears, but started gears.
I manufacture my thoughts in poetic form.
In the face of others, I try my best not to bite my tongue on complaints.
Better yet, lament although I am still not content.
It beats explosive, extensive tantrums.
As I look back, my products did not hinder my reason.
I have many concerns.
It is almost like a lifelong burden.

The last thing I'll do is pull a curtain.

Thankful

I am glad I have my caring elders.
I am happy I have a comfortable mattress.
I have a clean house,
Adequate technology,
A healthy body free from many complications and allergies.
I am satisfied with the way I look.
My day-to-day life is filled with a lot of conveniences.
I bring a lot of honor.
I have the pleasure of learning as much as I can handle.
I have the ability to meet many amazing people.
My worries vary, but less in comparison to many.

Lust

Lust can take away common sense.
Reason can fall to depths below a dark ocean.
This is just as bad as anger, maybe worse.
Some of the poorest decisions arise.
In these dark depths lives tunnel visions.
The scope of your lenses will widen when consequences come.
Diseases and viruses are big eye-openers.
A child or children may bring new parents from sleep.
We learn who are good and bad parents.
Lessons should not be hard to learn.
Hard learned lessons will bring reason when reason is gone.

Godless

No god, the ruler is God.

Rule and worship become one.

If there is nothing higher than that person

Dictatorship and free reign.

Brainwashing is easy, you see what I want you to see.

Serve me to receive the best life.

Serve me, our country can go to greater heights.

Your life is important, but I come first.

I am your religion.

We are intolerant of outsiders.

History is what I design it.

My Word

Five years ago, the teacher asked some questions.
Where do you see yourself in five years?
I am glad to say the vision is clear.
Things are more often closer than they appear.
What are your goals for five years?
I am pleased to say that they are completed, largely.
I do what I say.
It was hard, but I had plenty of time to play.
Find your lane and embrace it.
The pieces just fell into place.

Purpose

Some looked for answers,

Some followed their gut,

Some did what they liked,

Some stuck to a hobby,

Some made the right choice,

Some made some bad choices,

Some have strong conviction,

Some follow faith,

Some acted on hardship,

Some followed morality,

Some are talented,

Some use their talents,

Some got lucky.

Anger

When I take away your peace,

Believe your price is less.

Take it to greater heights and you'll shorten your given life lease.

I can leave a crease in your memory.

Make space for me.

I can make it hard to sleep at night.

Keep it up, you will be miserable for good.

Don't put yourself in a well.

I hope that is well understood?

Perspective is connected to feeling.

Think ahead of time, you might see it coming.

Make it a challenge, like a game.

It is not a bluff, I'm here.

Expression

Reading a face without expression,

It is like trying to interpret a page without words.

Words can be deceptive.

Nothing can be uttered.

We have to watch our behavior.

Threats

You think your threats can damage me.
You threaten me with therapy.
Taking in a threat is not a therapy itself.
It just allows me to remove a calmness from my hill.
A hill of emotions made of stones.
Walks help clear my mind.
I do not escape, but I get rid of.
I skip the bad ones across the lack of emptiness.
A string tied to dead weight will limit my progress.
This is like progress to me.
I have many connections to open many doors.
I am okay with this door shut.
You have to keep your mind clean.
Adding dirt to your day-to-day can make you filthy.

Daily Walks

On my walk from class, I ate Mediterranean food
Carrying a heavy bag in my dobok.
There was a woman talking to her phone in front of her door on a porch.
Each step I took, my bag would "clack" and "clink"
I was hungry, the spoon scraped the bowl between every bite.
The woman broke her neck to look back.
Her face gave the same expression first-timers give Casper.
She turned around, opened the screen door then shut it as she walked in.
While locking it, she gave a fearful look.
I am used to "this" uniform she just produced.
The kicker is I usually get that response when I wear something casual.
The typical cross the street, casual.
The neck breakers give you a, "why are you here?" look.
The concern is "What is he doing?" look.
Sometimes it is a different kind of look.
Usually when I am in a suit or dobok,
The question turns into a statement: "I didn't know they did that" look.
I get more head knobs, smiles and greetings from passing strangers.
Occasionally a hand clapped shut gesturing a prayer preceded by a bow.
On top of some random cliche phrase.

They probably never did that for anyone else a day in their life.

Normally they walk by with a nervous look.

Honesty

Honestly, honesty may not be the best policy.
Many reject the truth that is true.
Expose honesty in a life and you might be disliked for life.
A closed door can be like a muzzle.
It is done out of spite for a small slight.
A lie is worse,
A fancy world looks better than this one.
A lie is an insult to the autonomous.
What I say might lead to a bad day.
Or a day of grace.

Shape

We are shaped by the world around us.

What we bring to the table,

How we act,

Our consistency will shape progress.

Progress is a rise in economic status, social status, and moral status.

Waiting does not fix any issues, action does.

We wait and more die.

We wait and still, most are ignorant.

We wait and more suffer.

We wait and atrocities happen.

What is relevant to us can help us rise or fall.

Where is your passion?

What are your goals?

What are you working on?

Are goals being completed and crossed off?

Were you a good human being today?

Ruling Class

They have a great strategic ploy.

They can turn a variety of thoughts into only one.

There are many control methods, but desire is number one.

Religion or belief might be two.

These two are typically ubiquitous.

Rule by terror or let terror happen

At times, a rule by strength is obsolete.

Sometimes they will have to be a bit discrete to keep the peace.

A population's cathexis on desire is the worst.

These people tend to be manipulated first.

They stomp, kick and trample the rest.

Ancient Giver

The extremely passionate believe in providing for all, over gain.

When it is tit for tat, some expect nothing.

Some expect something back.

Those situations can forge a bond or open a crack.

I always wondered why some are free and some make a fee.

The former has a sense of purity; the other appears broke.

This one led them to tautology; the latter was seen as impure.

One looked disgusted at the other while the other laughed.

The difference is, some names live for thousands of years and others fade.

Modern Blues

You played a song from your phone,
We listened and pinpointed a particular line.
At that time, we were oblivious and frankly pretty careless.
People that make art always expose their hearts.
Some years later, it just hit me; this guy is letting out his pain too.
He mentioned suicide and while examining his life from my lens, it made sense.
One-on-one conversations tell me pain has not been dealt with.
Anger and sadness.
All the smoke and liquor, I did not see until now.
I felt like carelessness added to it.
The bystander did nothing about it.
I examine a lot of the songs and they meet a similar end.
A lot of them are sad and troubled.
Today, I listened to blues like Billie Holiday and B.B. King.
It is the stuff we like most or at least most attractive.
The best of the best have figured that out.

Busy

I'm never too busy.
My time is plentiful and flexible.
An hour to myself can be an hour to anyone else.
Relaxing might be a service to another.
Who's to say service to another isn't relaxation.
Too busy wasting time on using up time on nothing at all.
There is a lot of space in your day for doing nothing.
We always have time, but I don't have to prove anything.
I let the images speak for themselves.
Media time can be used to improve self might.
Burnout does not exist in me.
I must have figured out my self-care.
Regardless of that, I have a side tangent.
You can chase more rabbits Elmer Fudd.
Try to get more hits than 47.
You look silly letting those rabbits take your focus
That is child's play and it'll kill you slowly.
Wasted time makes up most of the landfills on earth.
Take a break to make some mental space.
Dwelling is self-induced anxious medalling.
Worry will turn clear skies into a flurry.
Let this live in your head rent-free.
Work to work less; that'll work for me.

Generation Gifts

Generational wealth of ignorance.
Parents or guardians are our first teachers and greatest influencers.
If you do not know, then advice is better unsaid.
Sharecropping told us debt is not the move.
Teach them about money.
If you don't know, don't go to the broke.
The kids are not assets or piggy banks.
Neither guilt you can fill up.
If you do it enough, they will harm themselves.
Even harm others.
Recycles plastic pain bottles refilled with bad suggestions.
Teach the proper identity; improve self-esteem and pride.
Educate them, but leave them to choose.
Do not omit your flaws and faults from them.
Your negative perception of your hair should not go to your kids.
If your pigment is horrific, then do not scar theirs.
Destructive habits do not have to be hidden but acknowledged.
Treatment, attitudes and thoughts towards others
Is probably the invisible elephant in the room.
Pass on honesty,
Pass on a tradition of accountability,
Pass on different perseverance,
Pass on a willingness to learn.

What's Up

When there is good news, usually the conversation is short.

When the news is bad, they want all the tea.

I cannot tell if they are more interested in my joy or pain.

Even if it was pain, trials and tribulation lead me to be the best of the best.

Achievement is intentional.

I call it finesse.

Coping

Tests used to bother me like I was on my fourth-second guess.

I watch comedy to relax myself.

Part of coping is preparation.

Payments are not such a bother if I do not have a lot of them.

When any storm passes, make a good habit of any action to deal with the aftermath.

If it is easy and detrimental, it is problematic.

Old Strangers

As we aged, there was a change;
Changes in eye contact.
Less waving.
Conversations became shorter.
Paths in life split up.
I'm reading about achievement.
I don't see myself living for recognition and compliments.
I reconnected with an old friend and not much changed
Some days passed.
I'm Sipping from a mug and looking at a mugshot.
In terms of life, some moved up, stayed or moved down.
I realized over time there is a hierarchy to life.
I believe I moved up, but don't trip over anything you will not bleed for.
I have to be for myself.

Inner circle

I crossed a lot of people to reach this point.

It is almost like I am appointed.

So it's hard to get anointed.

Regardless, it took a village to make a mind like this.

A community to form this mouthpiece.

Pieces fall into place as if it was destined.

Opportunity

I take everything that comes my way.

Anyone that stands in my way will have something good to pay.

The devil got off my shoulder a while ago.

Or maybe just a part of me.

A creative, analytical mind is what opportunity brings.

Success is constantly on my mind.

I see a great life in my visions, it's a purposeful methodical process.

I do not feel like I am taking all the opportunities I could have.

Like taking the opportunity to visit more.

Maybe some more phone calls would bring us a little closer.

Maybe talking more before passing would have helped me handle grief and closure.

When we are on the phone, all we discuss is my life exposure.

The rugrats need a model, but I'm not around.

I was told they are not my responsibility.

You have a lot going on, so focus on yourself.

In a sense, I feel like I let them down.

It is hard to talk to them, that is my disconnect.

Not a signal my antennas are picking up.

Too busy to keep all my promises.

People over progress was my mist opportunity.

Belittle The Bad

My uncle said, do not make the past a weapon.

Do not talk down because pumping filth into his head won't bring good.

In fact, it will only reinforce it.

It can bring worse parts of history to the future.

Listen to it too much, you will take it in and believe it to be true.

Self-esteem and self-worth get paper-thin.

Do not get me wrong, they do wrong.

Acting as if they do no wrong is like putting them in a fantasy land.

The truth sucks frankly.

No surprise, facts become opinions when they do not like the truth.

The truth is, he listens to the bad double the amount he listens to the good.

Be the person he can get guidance from instead of a tongue lashing.

Celebrate

He asked why I do not celebrate.

I did not have a good answer for him.

I said I have a lot of accomplishments and more to come.

Then it clicked for me.

Life has been great with its heavy challenges, but uncertain.

I guess there is a part of me waiting for a reward.

I'm waiting for it all to be said and done.

I am unsure of when to call it.

I think another part of me is expecting disappointment.

What is all the praise for if the result is nothing

And who's to say I am progressing or not

At times I feel like the praise is fake.

Sometimes the praise is not to do with me, but them.

Spoken Word and Poetry

Watching and listening to spoken word is one of my favorite pastimes. Spoken word to me is the implementation of aspects of (verbal and instrumental) music, poetry and physical expression.

Comfort In Weather

I wanted to get away.
You're so, so attractive.
Physical affection is what keeps me drawn. (Hug yourself)
We are at war with trauma.
I unsheath my weapon (remove sword)
I'm a pretty good ARTIST! (Air draw with pen)
I can make a timid dog dance to the BANG of thunder.
Help a scared child see the awe in fireworks.
I'll help you love rainy days.
I have a pretty good rain dance. (Two step)
I can't take away pain
Like precipitation, it's always recurring.
I LOVE you and I really LOVE your mama.
Well, I haven't defined it yet, but I'll find out.
Lighting is like Drama.
A cloudy day can leave people with nebulous thoughts.
But I can help you see the sunshine (squint).
And you look good in all dim lighting.
The atmosphere could be black as a crow and you're still a great image (cover your eyes).

I’ve seen your mind and I almost went blind
You know you’re really bright. (point to head).
No tornado, hurricane, earthquake, tsunami,
landslide...micro-climate change
Could tear how I feel about you apart.
But please, fix yourself before you rip my heart apart.

Tight Grip

That GOD talk was boring sometimes.

I slept standing with my eyes open. (Close eyes) (Drowsy Stance)

When standing at times, I almost fell OVER! (trip and wipe mouth)

Your talk helped me all over. (Open arms wide)

YOU TAUGHT ME TO NEVER ROLL OVER!

Looking back; looking forward….

Your words were and still are my four-leaf clover.

Everyone has a timer.

I'm selfish as hell, so you know if you die...

I.. I'll come to heaven and drag you back down. (dragging)

You went through a lot of hell.

I could only wish I gave you heaven here.

I cried a million times and still, I can't hold the tears back. (wipe your eyes)

I thought letting loose meant lacking strength.

I held it till I exploded like an atomic bomb.

Cancer was my worst flipping enemy. (speak fast)

Excuse my language, I know you taught me better.

Forgive me, I know she taught me better. (Look up, speak low)

I don't have enemies.

The possibility of future mourn led me to anger in written form

She is the best blessing you could provide me.

I pray to extend timers.
One day I'll wear a fitting crown to make her proud.
All I want her to see is that her life lessons helped a baby become king
Thank you, these tears feel good now.

In My Head

If you think badly of yourself,
Think three good thoughts of yourself.
But, why not more?
Today, I felt worse than I ever felt before. (hang head low)
Well yesterday, but I still feel it.
It didn't go my way.
Like basketball players that DIDN'T! go by play
Mentally!, physically!, emotionally! I'm drained today.
(Gesture being drenched)
On a blue day, it helps to have healthy ways to remove the color.
There are many ways to deal with the pain.
Some things we are unable to get away from.
I told myself you have done so much good in life.
Look at all the trouble you helped people get away from.
Look at the smiles you've helped make on many faces.
(smile)
You're so unique. (Point out to people)
Who else thinks like you?
You don't lie in your smile. (Smile)
Every second your growth shows.
Almost every hour, you bloom that much more. (Gesture Index and thumb close)
Your mentality keeps you away from certain doom.
You've persevered through mountain heavy challenges.
Even if you're looked at in the eyes of a few bad others,

All the love you give to others,

All hate you give yourself,

Tell yourself how much you love yourself more often.

M.W.M.N.

From spiders, ants, praying mantis, silverfish, and centipedes.
(Count on fingers)
I murder so many insects.
From flowers, shrubs, trees, and weeds. (counts on fingers)
I've killed so much vegetation.
Nature's serial killer.
Me and many others are pillars that hold this title.
Pillars that hold up the destruction of mother nature.
We all play a part;
From athletic games to street lights, cars, cell phones and many more.
I could fit the list to match the amount of Harry Potter pages in all books. (open arms)
I think she's upset with us
But as we go, nature will rebuild and engulf our creation.
Reign supreme again.
The world is like one big house the human family lives in.
Some family members are less considerate of the home than others.
The landlord (mother nature) will soon evict families for the treatment of the home.
May heat rise to cook us in this big circular oven? (Index finger circle with on hand)
May water act as a giant cover?
Or a Number of disasters flatten places?
Diseases and viruses heighten.

Could the family be so angry we kill each other?

Would you trash your own house?

Treat the earth like the place you love most.

Coach

You helped a lot.
A- was never good enough.
You helped me through a lot of games.
If I was not doing right then, you're the first to know.
I let it be known,
Then my head would hang low.
The voice of disappointment caused a lot of sorrow.
Not only sorrow but drive every time I walked out, my chin was up.
I channeled that energy to further my progress.
Your words stuck, I think of them when I'm out of luck.
Sometimes life sucks.
You always had a phrase to keep me up.
My achievements blew up.
My self-esteem blew up.
Become so strong, you can't go corrupt.
Work differently, not hard.
Realize you have the quality of leaders to lead.
Be like a bird feeder.
Let everyone come to you for nourishment and
Supply to all without discrimination.
They have become better from it.
That's a piece of what makes you unique.
They come to pick your mind and acknowledge your thoughts.

Music

Just sit back, it can relax.
It comes in many and any form.
Borrow some peace or make a violent beast.
Be careful what you listen to.
It can even be a saw sworn to scorn and scold. (Frown)
It can promote drugs.
It can add the finishing touch to produce a bully. (Make a fist)
It can show love through hugs (hug gestures) and kisses.
It can comfort in agony and maybe the therapy needed.
Despair could headline every verse.
It can inspire, (lift arms) and be relatable.
Or non-existent in your world.
One can listen to an entire song and not know a word.
Music can form goals and influence achievement.
You can hear good or evil. (lift and hold both hands)
Listen to things that can elevate.
Whether a space shuttle or a realization never aware of before.
The trap, guns, psychedelics will lead you to slump.
Petty talk exposes good panhandlers. (hold out hands)
Progressive talk brings leaders. (cheesy superman pose)

One Over Many

We had a talk.

He started off by saying “look I got a lot”.

I replied, “I only have one, so I can’t relate”.

He asked, “how she is?”

I say, “a little rocky, but we’ll be alright.”

He said, “I do not have those problems.”

I exclaimed, “I suppose, but you have a bigger problem within yourself.”

“I am not here to compete.”

He quietly said, “Why love or care so much? There are so many ups and downs it is so cyclical.”

“It is as if you are both on a seesaw with hula hoops.”

I quietly replied, “if you only focus on reaching the highest heights, you would not know how many times your feet hit the ground.”

“Sometimes the seesaw is imaginary. At times the downs should not be seen as downs.”

He said with a sigh, “whatever, I get lots of love.”

I gave a light laugh “At least I know when she says she loves me, I know she means it.”

Haiku

Haiku is interesting to me for many reasons. A haiku style of poetry is short yet very descriptive. Haiku can be insightful with imagery. The messages from these people can be highly impactful. The quiet person does not talk much, but when that person talks, keep an open ear.

Medication

Floating white petals,
Calmness reigns all over me,
Graceful dance of grass.

Fishing

Many fish in sight,
Water's clarity, pure as birth.
Without a tug, I achieve patience.

Challenges

Dislikeable people,
Bullies are an obstacle,
I learn tolerance.

Differences

Guidance led to more,
I listen to my elders,
It created space.

Same

If stolen from,
If I chose to steal back once,
I am just alike.

Closed Open Doors

Rejection happens
For a thousand seals over me,
Finally a yes.

Circle

Our day to day
Like a clock tick tock, time moves,
Eyes, little changes.

Beach

Soft, small, bright tan sands
Bright, blue loud waving oceans
My tranquility.

Stories

Stories are a great way to learn lessons. I think stories are powerful, inspiring, and develop uneasiness. People will begin to realize that they are not the only ones going through hardship. Stories can promote a perception change. Telling your story can keep someone out of trouble, reduce their worry, and keep them going when they do not want to. These stories are scenarios in my life that I am grateful to share.

Effort

I had extra time away from school because of my leg injury. My performance in school was not ideal. I needed work, particularly in reading and writing. I struggled most in those aspects of education. There is a negative stain on your self-confidence. You could imagine the stress spike from popcorn reading. There is a weight of anxiety when we read each other's writings. Grammar was an uphill battle for a long while. I also avoided reading my work. I think part of the reason for this is the acknowledgement of my mistakes. I would rather have been completely devoid of fault than think about corrections. My mother decided to get me into tutoring services. I was playing football at the time for the middle school Tigers team. After football practice in middle school, my mother suggested I receive a tutoring service. Looking back, she worked full-time with two sons at a job she would rather not be in. She would usually handle some other business when I was dropped off. After a long hour and a half of reading, mom would pick me up. She always identified areas I needed aid. I was encouraged to read books and supplemented writing guides. I was not having it because games were much more fun. I wish I did read a bit more. If I took advantage of reading books, I would have prevented a lot of mess.

Lesson turmoil

I was teaching martial art techniques to this young individual. His younger brother was rambunctious and very lively. The younger brother would run around tossing the hula hoop and try to get my attention. I think that was all he wanted, attention. I tried to get him involved in the lesson so maybe he would simmer down. I tried my best to get his attention, but it was not working. The older brother was trying to do the same. After a few moments, I decided to ignore and continue the lesson. When I did, the brother would come for a moment and try to get involved. He had a bag of pretzels in his hand. The pretzel bags can be noisy and distracting. I politely suggested he put them to the side. He refused, so I suggested he put it in his pocket, then he became willing to cooperate. His pockets were not big enough, so the older brother took the bag and tried to put it off to the side. The younger brother became upset and walked away. Someone new had come into the room, so I gave more attention to that person so she was caught up. While I turned away from the brothers, they had a small altercation. The younger brother was on the floor whining and the older one was standing. I assumed he pushed him to the ground. I told the older brother to sit down with authority. I let the younger brother keep to himself. He bounced back up and decided to walk away once more. I brought my attention back to the newcomer. When I finished the update, I went to the older brother. I told him all the advice and moral application I can muster. I was trying to give him what I did not get at his age. The two were both in the wrong, but with age comes responsibility. When I saw the older brother, I saw myself. I just wanted him to avoid my mistakes with my younger brother. I wish I could go back in time. I have apologies I have not gotten to yet.

Council

I did poorly on my second biology exam. I was upset and a little panicked. I wanted to boost the grade so badly. My spirit had become low. I went to the professor's office during office hours for help. As we were going through the exam, she noticed my uneasiness. She said, "Dorian, this is a small piece of your life. You will not remember this in forty years." I said "true, but if I keep this up I will be bald in forty days."

Alternative Focus

When I started school, I was so intent on getting school work done well. A 4.0 is what I strived for like any student. I also loved going to the gym. At the gym, I got to release tension through basketball and workouts. My body was and still is great, of course. I had the pleasure of meeting a lot of cool people. Eventually, I found my first girlfriend and I was so happy. She desired my presence, but I came first. I wanted her to be happy, so I took time out to be around her more. She was already happy; just think of it like icing on the cake. I enjoyed it, but a piece of me is missing. I couldn't help thinking about what I could have been doing if I was not around her. This book, exercise, and school work. Her mother asked if I had homework or something to study for. I managed my time well for school, so it was not a big deal. Another benefit to being around her was the animals. A black cat with yellowish-green eyes and a brown Shih Tzu. I did not have a dog or cat, but I wanted them. She would complain "they were more important than me." I said, "I agree, blame my mother's allergies." In addition, in my later years of school, I decided maybe I should not have any animals. I got to know her mom and she would make dinner for us. The girlfriend expressed her happiness towards me coming around. She would say "You see this mom, he is where he's supposed to be!" Her mother quietly replied, "You're making him lazy."

Raking

I went to my grandmother's house to rake leaves. She offered to pay, but I did not want to take the money. I always felt as if payment was something taboo. This is my family after all; therefore, I should not be paid to do it. I receive a great greeting and a lot of love. After some catching up, I got to rake leaves. This rake is old, it is the same one I have been using since I could rake. It was a bit therapeutic because I was not burdened by my personal concerns. It was a windy, chilly day. My grandparents have a lot of big trees around their house. The trees' colors were vibrant reds and yellows. Fall is one of my favorite seasons because of all the crippling, dying leaves. As I was scrapping leaves up into piles, I got a small brown rectangular trash can close by. I used the clear bags they gave me to hold the leaves. I used a shovel to pick it up and place it into the trash can. Eventually, I took the bag of leaves out, filled it with more leaves then tied it up. Shortly after, my great-grandmother comes from the house and asks if I want some help. I said, "no, I got this, don't worry about it." She asked, "are you sure?". Of course I need help. This pile is intimidating. I also had some work to do when I got back home. She said "Alright, I'll tell your grandmother he said he did not need any help" in a jokingly, sarcastic tone. I just did not see a reason for a woman almost 90 to be outside bothering with this. I continued gathering more leaves to the pile. I opened a second bag up, placed it in the trashcan and got to business. Halfway through, she came back outside to offer some help again. She says "Let me help you, you have more important things to do than bother with this. Here, I will hold the bag… (as I was filling the bag she added). Look, you'll be here all day picking this stuff up." I was hesitant for a second, but I broke and agreed. I placed leaves into the bag while some tears dropped down my face. Part of it was pride; the other part was that I did not want her to do it. Being the manly man I am, I tried to hide it. I do not think she noticed the tears. As we finished filling and tying the bags, I placed them side by side in a row. The first bag, my bag, was the smallest and took the most time. With her help, I filled the bags faster and the bags were even bigger.

Sewage

One morning, I woke up to a flooded basement floor with sewage. When I told my mother, she became frantic. She wanted me to investigate the situation. Anything from the main pump will never have a great smell. (I did not know it was the main pump at the time) I grabbed some old boots and took a look. After some searching, I found out that the cap from a tube in the ground was off. When water ran, it would flow through that hole. We figured something was clogging the tube, presumably tissue. After some thought, my mother couldn't come to a good solution to this issue. After some talking, it was put on me, but I knew no better than her. She told me to get to the hardware store for something to cover the tube. We did not know what we were looking for. After some confusing conversations with tradespeople, they asked some questions and I answered as best I could. Luckily, I had some pictures taken on my phone before I left. They were able to see and told me it was the main pump. The current cap did not fit anymore, so we had to measure the original cap for a better fit. We found a replacement, it almost fit, but it was not sufficient. As time went on, mom's emotions were a bit more tense, understandably so. Money is tight and this is an unfortunate circumstance. I went back to another closer hardware store for a better cap. I and a worker there went through a less confusing conversation. The worker offered a cap and a brush to clean the gunk off of the lining for the thread to twist onto. Brushing did not do much good, but it brought a more unpleasant smell. I made another trip back to the hardware store and they mentioned a snake. I could rent or buy; for one-time use, it is better to rent. I called my mother and told her about the snake. She did not know what to do with it; neither did I. There was a great level of concern and worry. The person who recommended a snake knew we were amateurs. He asked me rhetorically with a smile "You do not know what you're doing with that do you?" I laughed and said, "I sure don't". He replied, "Let me give you a number to the plumber. You'll mess up the pipes if you do not know what you're doing." I waited for him to ring up the plumber. He eventually got in contact so we can trade contacts. One thing I had learned there was that it is better to seek as much advice as possible than go blindly into something I knew nothing about. I avoided a few hundred dollars on a snake rental and useless caps. I went home and then called the plumber to explain the situation. Before he came to the house, my brother and I had to move some things around. One of the house rules is no shoes in the house. She does not want dirt or whatever else will be tracked on the floors. After some plumbing investigation, moving and snaking the problem was solved. He said, "get a plastic cap that can fit over the exposed hole. It was a bit tough dealing with this." In certain circumstances, I wish I had more guidance. I was put into a position in which I needed different shoes to walk in.

Class Problems

I had a friend in the early days of high school tell me about his experience in history class. He and his classmates watched a film on slavery and emancipation. In terms of the class, the demographic can be compared to a black dot on a white sheet of paper. He was the dot. There was a discussion afterwards about the film. The discussion focused on progress (at least the appearance of it) and the troubles the freedmen went through. Hardship and maltreatment were heavy during these times. Other students would laugh during the film and often look back at him. When questions came during the discussion the non-students of color were hesitant. They were fearful of saying the wrong thing. All eyes were on the dot like they were watching the first person go on an obstacle course. Apparently, he knows the course best. Subjects like this are needed and acceptable.

Damnatio Memoriae

I found myself pondering things I'm not used to pondering. Thinking about it made me a little sour. The more I think about it, the more it sticks then the worse it gets. I scroll through social media viewing videos and photos of distasteful things. There are messages in all the content we view. I had to get rid of some people because they were not conducive to progress or becoming happier. Through ignorance and gullibility, people believe in appearances. Mental fortitude, resilience and wisdom can combat this. By depriving ourselves of the negative thoughts we get rid of filth. We may have to stop affiliation with certain groups and or change what we search. Change the algorithm of your day-to-day focus. I work to reduce the negative thoughts in my life. The ones by my side are the ones I want around me rather than the ones that are just around me.

Friends

In fifth grade, during recess, a group of the usuals wanted to play football on a field by the playground. They were picking people and I did not make the cut. I was upset by the selection process. I watched for a little then I decided to go into the playground areas. Visibly upset, the teacher had shown some concern. She asked what was wrong and I explained the issues I had. She explained I did not have to hang around them. If they do not want you around then, do not hang around them. Some of them are trouble and you should stay away. Make different friends with the people that want to be around you. When I was younger, my father would always say “do not hang around the wrong crowd.”

Small

She said there is a difference between men and women. I could not defend myself if I tried. I replied, if insects knew how scared we can be of them, imagine the power they would have. She said, Insects do not have power. I exclaimed, well, look at bees and wasps, if one were to fly around anyone's face, the person would move frantically. The bee is small, but there is a specific noise, there is a weapon, their stingers. You see it all the time grown men run from bees. They have a reputation; not individually, but rather as a collective. Think of every spider people avoid and run from. There is a certain paranoia associated with them. The words spider, bees and wasps alone will bring fear. They have a certain tenacity, viciousness, ferociousness and reputation in their arsenal. Cats can be very cuddly, they sit on your lap so you can pet them. When anyone reaches the wrong place or pets them in a way they dislike, then blood is drawn. After that interaction, the owner would second guess petting the cat again. There are warning signs they give and tolerance for certain actions are strict. Wash them with soap and water if you dare. It does not matter if you hand raise them. There is the long-running joke about the elephants' fear of mice. Go get appropriate weapons, be stern in what you allow from someone, improve your mind, and enhance your physical condition. Know when to turn on the kill switch like a tiger or hit the button to speed off like a cheetah.

Ungrateful

I thought about all the things I take for granted. The fact that I have a bed. The amount of and type of clothing I have. I take for granted the amount and type of shoes I have. I take for granted the people that care for and about me. As I ran through that list I sank into amazement. The list is a lot bigger than I thought. Sometimes I do not make good use of my free time. I take for granted the heat, electricity, running water, and wifi. After watching a war happening on TV, I realized how fast everything can go away. During my time teaching I met a young girl whose family was running from terror. My professor talked about people in the middle east trying to ride the wings of planes from horrific military control. Outside of that, a sudden health condition can flip anyone's world. I did not realize how beautiful walking is until I had to teach myself how to walk again. In some ways, it changed the trajectory of my life. Every action, possession, or word could be our last action at any moment.

Perspectives

I had a justice related conversation with some young people about the stuff I have going on in my life. All the accomplishments and goals I have. I addressed my likes and dislikes. I consider myself an introverted person. I am not one to go out to parties. Frankly, I had never been to one. I am not one to drink and smoke either. I just said it is not my flavor. I tell them I take pleasure in reading, learning new things, enjoying a good movie, exercising, playing games, martial arts, the list goes on. The responses I got were boring, surprised looks, and genuine interest. Some considered me to be an old man or to act like one because that doesn't seem to be what young people do. A young man from an urban setting in America is outside of the "norm", especially a young black man, wide nose, big lips, and locked coiled hair. The same features that led my mother to explain why they look at us differently as we grew older. The same reason my brother came expressing a complaint. While walking down a street a few houses down, a neighbor said, "nice shoes, your parents must be drug dealers." I went on a tiny tangent after that story. Sooner or later, anything gets tired of being poked. Treat people the way you want to be treated. What do you do when everyone doesn't follow that rule? I told them about moving a certain way to make a good standing, but also moving in a way to where their perspective changes about us. Moving forward, I had a conversation with a professor (an actual old man) after class. He asked me what I will do over the spring break. I told him all that I have going on and he seemed surprised, even delighted. I ended up learning a lot more about him. We talked about poetry and martial arts, and some outside work as well. He praised me and said "I am happy that you are doing what you are doing. Taking advantage of the time you have by using it to get what you want out of the way. There will be a certain point where you'll have to pay bills and put food on the table. You won't have as much time as you do now. You'll be better set for the future and without regret, wishing you could have done whatever when you were younger. A lot of these young people waste it."

None the wiser

My mother came downstairs one day and asked if I knew about a particular topic. It was some random fact people usually do not know. I knew the answer and what she was about to say, but I was curious. I said, "I don't know." She went on to explain the particular topic. At the end, she said "isn't that surprising I did not know that?" I said "I knew", her face changed from happy to confused. She said, "If you knew that then, why did you say "I don't know." I replied, "I wanted to learn something new. There might have been something I missed."

About The Author

Dorian Scott Withrow Jr. was born on April 13th, 2000, in Buffalo, New York. His education primarily was fundamentally through the Amherst central school district. Dorian began his blossoming in high school by facing and conquering many challenges. His achievements were within many programs he was involved in. Programs such as Youth of the Year, Jack and Jill of America, Leadership Buffalo, and

Breaking Barriers. He was accepted into Canisius College in 2018, majored in ABEC Animal Behavior Ecology and Conservation with a minor in Philosophy. Throughout college Dorian was still involved in Breaking Barriers attending meetings, participating in activism and doing podcasts. He was also involved in his newly found passion, ITF Taekwondo. Dorian graduated from Canisius college in May 2022.

Youth of the year (Boys and Girls Club)

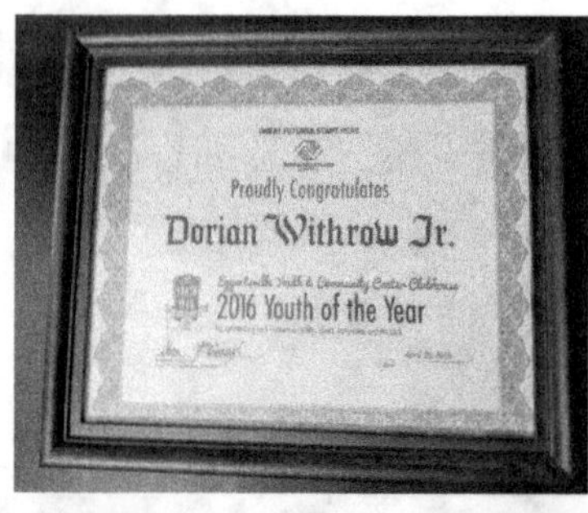

Youth of the Year is an achievement that youth in Boys and Girls clubs accomplish for community involvement, leadership, character, and even mentorship for younger people. People who receive this honor not only receive recognition but have the opportunity to move on to greater milestones. Youth members selected from different Boys and Girls Clubs around the city are offered to take part in different workshops to meet the next stage. Workshops like public speaking, writing, teaching, etc. He did not meet the next stage, but out of six competitors, he came in second.

Jack & Jill Of America

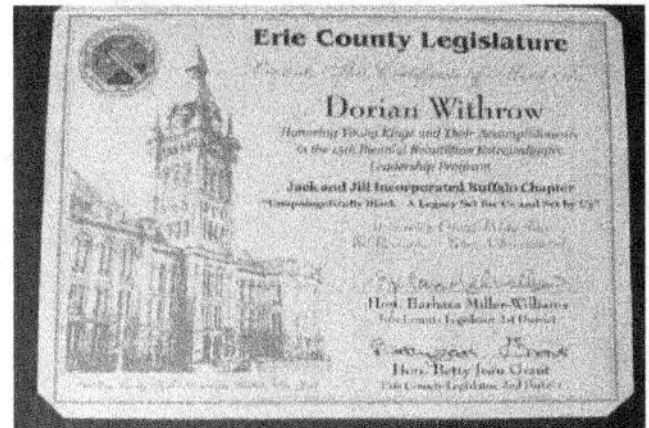

Dorian was also involved in Jack & Jill of America, a program for young black males. The program held many workshops such as leadership, fitness, dress to impress, public speaking, and dance (West African and Urban Ballroom). This program allowed for the creation of a network among its members. Community service was another element of the program to instill the importance of serving Exposure to many unique people and aided Dorian in character development. At the end of the program, boys become men through African rights of passage. The final ceremony involved our speeches, dance, and rights of passage. The boys got to give themselves a name when they became men. Dorian Became Adwin (thinker and artist).

Leadership Buffalo

Leadership Buffalo, Inc.

This certificate signifies that

Dorian Withrow

has successfully completed all requirements of Leadership Buffalo's Youth Leadership Program Class of 2017

LEADERSHIP BUFFALO
Making Buffalo Better

Leadership buffalo was a program Dorian experienced during his first retreat. He met a lot of interesting people from special backgrounds. Leadership Buffalo also held a lot of workshops regarding leadership, cooking, dining etiquette

(Lesson from a former butler of the queen of England), diversity, inclusion and more. There was an amazing opportunity for teamwork and building more connections.

Honors and Rewards

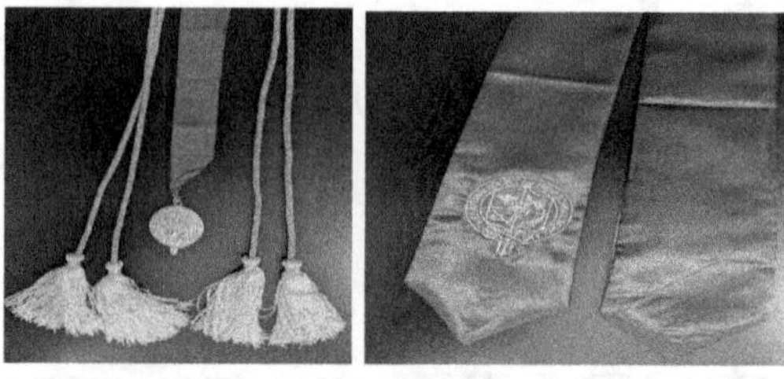

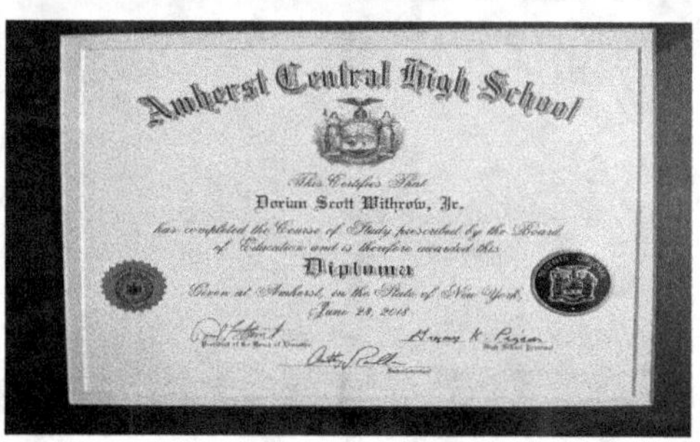

Dorian received many honors and rewards in high school. Dorian obtained the national honors society for maintaining merit roll in high school. He also attended Harkness Erie One Boces for Animal Science and earned national technical honors society. Dorian gained scholarships from Buffalo Urban League and Delta Sigma Theta Sorority. Finally, he graduated from high school in 2018 and pursued a bachelor's at Canisius College. As of now he is a Canisius alumni with a bachelor in science. Dorian had a strong liking for philosophy. His love for philosophy has led him to earn a place in Phi Sigma Tau, a Philosophical honor society and be rewarded with St. Thomas Aquinas Award in Philosophy for having demonstrated exceptional achievement in philosophy. Lastly, the Martin Luther King Award for promoting social justice, social harmony, civil rights, human rights, advocacy of the poor and non-violence.

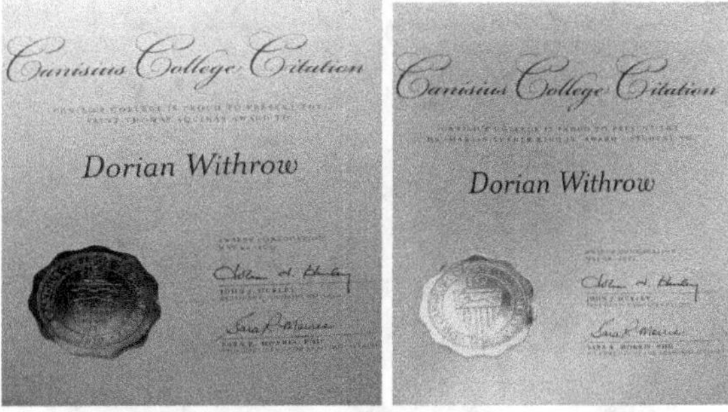

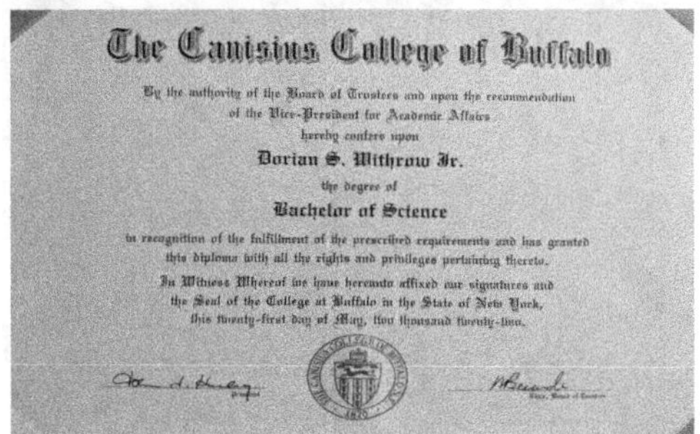

The Canisius College of Buffalo

By the authority of the Board of Trustees and upon the recommendation of the Vice-President for Academic Affairs hereby confers upon

Dorian S. Withrow Jr.

the degree of

Bachelor of Science

in recognition of the fulfillment of the prescribed requirements and has granted this diploma with all the rights and privileges pertaining thereto.

In Witness Whereof we have hereunto affixed our signatures and the Seal of the College at Buffalo in the State of New York, this twenty-first day of May, two thousand twenty-two.

Dorian is a graduate and still a youth council member of Breaking Barriers, a program in which males of color ages twelve to twenty four, act on policy, mentoring, leadership, and improving work opportunities and conditions of other young people in education. (just to name a few.). Dorian gained very valuable knowledge and developed many meaningful connections. Dorian has had the opportunity to become a social justice trainer and continues to engage in the Breaking Barriers podcasts.

BREAKING BARRIERS

Certificate of Completion

THIS CERTIFIES THAT

Dorian Withrow

Has completed one year of service as a member of the Breaking Barriers Youth Leadership Council - Cohort #1 and satisfied the necessary requirements of The My Brother's Keeper - Boys and Men of Color Initiative.

This 19th day of January 2019

Racial Equity Roundtable

Community Foundation

ITF Taekwondo

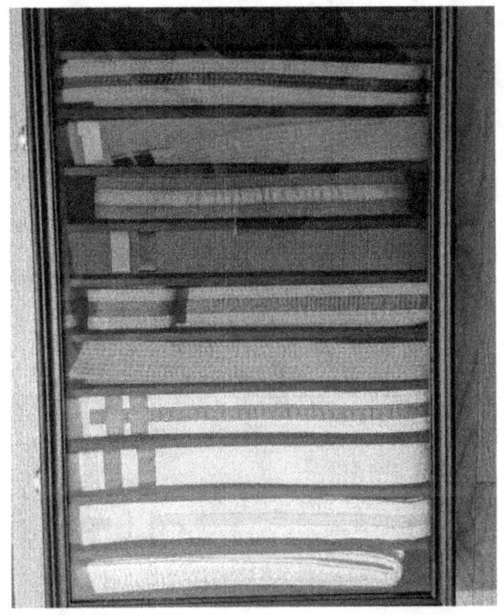

Dorian is also a martial artist and ITF Taekwondo practitioner. He has some knowledge of Isshin Ryu karate from his grandfather. Dorian Started ITF Taekwondo in May 2019. Through diligent and persistent work, he achieved a master's club affiliation. He also takes part in D.E.L.TA. Team (dedicated enthusiastic, loyal, teaching, assistant) where he can assist in teaching and uplifting others' lives. Dorian is officially a Cho Dan and passionate about further training.

Book Authored By Dorian S.Withrow Jr.

Book Alphabetical

Speak! Young Brown People, Speak. We are listening! A.L. Savvy Publications 2014, 2022

Wisdom 45 Advice Dorian S. Withrow Jr., Withrow LLC, Buffalo NY, 2022

www.ingramcontent.com/pod-product-compliance
Lightning Source LLC
Chambersburg PA
CBHW060531130626
46553CB00002B/713
* 9 7 9 8 9 8 6 5 2 3 8 0 4 *